The 77 Fragments of my LoveStory

Janelle Randall

The 77 Fragments of my LoveStory
Copyright © 2017 by Janelle Randall

Printed in USA by 48HrBooks (www.48HrBooks.com)

This book is dedicated
To the young girl who never felt loved
and always seemed so different.

Acknowledgements

I would like to take this opportunity to thank the many individuals who took the time out of their schedules in being available to me when I needed guidance, encouragement or simply a listening ear throughout my journey of writing this book. To all those who provided support, offered feedback, allowed me to quote their remarks and assisted in the editing, proofreading and design.

A special Thank you to Apostle Mark T. Jones Sr. , Lady Lisa Jones and Pastor Crystal Bailes for the impartation of wisdom, guidance and leadership in my life; as well as your dedication in cultivating the necessary components of learning one's purpose and God given design for their life. My life has been impacted by your influence. God bless you.

A special shout out to my family; I pray this book encourages you as much as it has encouraged me.

Above all, I would like to Thank my Lord and Savior Jesus Christ for giving his life to save a dark and wicked world for a time such as this.

I am honored to be a solider in your kingdom and I continually fall deeper in love with you as each day passes. Thank you for your provisions over my life and the divine calling you have placed on my life to impact others for your name's sake.

Foreword

Throughout the journey of this book
I have had ebbs and flows
somedays I wrote exceptionally, effortlessly
and on other days I became anxious to finish
and to just be done
I know however God has given me the instruction
for the completion of this book.
Somedays I read back on what I wrote
amazed at how I've overcome so much
and endured so many obstacles
realizing that God has kept me the entire time
for such a time as this.
I am honored and humbled to write this work for you
I know that it will set you free, as it has with me.
God bless you

Once upon a season
There once was a girl who sought to be loved
who sought to be kissed
who sought to be hugged
it began as a child,
she expected it from her mother
but her mother seemed cold
and wasn't capable
There once was a girl who sought to be valued
who sought attention
who needed appreciation
but that never came to pass
it started as a child
that girl became a young woman
and determined to move on
to seek the things she wanted
and to never look back
she always excelled
created many things
learned to be a boss
ministered to others out of that broken place and
assumed that because she covered the deep hole in her
soul with sod and fabricated green grass that life was
getting better

Who is Sade

Who is Sade?
do you know her?
have you seen her?
have you heard her?
Many have their opinions,
which are never really true
God forbid, if she didn't
know her
if she didn't , others lies
would be her reality
reality of self
i once read a quote that
said you create your own
reality with your
perspective
on another note,
some say she is a model
or should be a doctor
some say she is a mother
has 7 brothers
not counting her other
siblings from her fathers
side
some say she is an entrepreneur
a cook
homemaker
dream chaser
innovator
but what does she think?
everyone wants to know her, to be her, learn from her.
but what does she think?

Oceans
i love the sounds of waves crashing
the smell of salt water traveling back and forth upon
granules of sand
the infinite stars that overlook a black horizon
or the sun blazing upon my freckled body and face
at these times i reflect
on my day
life &
goals.

Pink and blue
hi pink
hi blue
i love you
pink i love the way you brighten my day
i endlessly dream of flowers
and any distress fades away
blue your sweet.
too sweet.
but i like you too
you remind me its ok to be masculine and hide my
innermost secrets with you
but pink, you bring me joy. like no other i could explain
and when i think of how ridiculous thats sounds i feel like
I've become chained
chained in your perfect
unconditional
unyielding
all encompassing
love.

Not allowed
Your not allowed to give up
your not allowed to tap out
There are others depending on you
waiting for your words of encouragement
your smile
and the grace you exhibit
Your not allowed.
Your not allowed to be arrogant
Your not allowed to be corrupt
there are cups to be filled
and you could never pour out
what you do not have.

Rain
Everyone knows when its raining
Many prepare for it
Many anticipate it
Many know that it comes in seasons
I've personally always loved the smell
the sound
I can hear it now
the sound of water drops beating against the ground
the cadence it creates
it is
unmistakably, undoubtedly
the sound of rain falling
I just love to watch the rain-fall
the sight is absolutely mesmerizing
my mind becomes still
and i take another deep breath
an enormous inhale
of the smell of
rain
sometimes i get chills
I become lost in the moment

WaterMelons

I overheard a story once
and this is how it went
There was a waitress
she had a few waitress
friends
she came in one day and
was unhappy
she was a gardener in her
spare time
you see she had been
nurturing this plant
that began as a
watermelon seed
she watched it grow
began to root
began to flourish
began to produce its fruit
she nourished it
watched over it
turned it regularly in the ground to prevent warping
but this particular day
it had disappeared
which was the cause of her sadness
she told her waitress friends
they encouraged her
said maybe someone who didn't have any food needed it
maybe an animal ate it
but wherever it was, whoever took it
probably needed it more than she did
several weeks later her husband mentioned giving it to his
mother
What if God had you nurture and care for something
that he intended for others to consume?

Roots
uprooted
from where i was planted
toppled over
barley standing
no longer to provide
habitation for those that
depended on me
uprooted
i saw what was beneath
Stagnant waters
beneath the surface
of who i use to be
funny how a storm can
uproot some of the most
buried things
unrevealed until the
remnants of what the storm tore up is exposed,
fears never confronted
memories unfold.

Sleepless

Tonight i feel as though
I can not sleep
My heart feels heavy
My tea has not steeped
Death is around us,
upon us at all times
I pray you have your assignment
Our Lord is so divine
We are in the labor pains of the last days
I've noticed the contractions
these words are not in vain
as each days passes
i realize that God's hands are upon me
I've been designed with purpose
as he had destined me to be
and when he is done using me,
I will go home to him forever
No one knows the day
of their last day of life
just as no one knows when he is returning

Wholeness

what is it?

W is for the washing, of the blood you had to forgo

h is for the hope you have in God and the added measure of Glory upon your life

o is for the observations you noticed in your life that needed to change

l is for the limitless heights you will go as you continue to press into who you really are

e is for experiencing the true power and identify of who you are and have been created to be
unapologetically

n is for never settling
never settling for the fake version of you that man tried to create

e is for errors God will reveal and heal in your process

s is for the symptoms you will start to have in response to birthing the idea God has placed in your heart

s is for saying YES to God's will and assignment

Untitled
There is a new place
Where God wishes for me to enter in
for some it is easy for others it can be quite slim
I have been called to love
to be loved
to experience love.
But I don't want to go
I make excuses
I attempt to runaway
Why?
Because I am fearful
I know and it is easy to recite
God does not give us a spirit of FEAR, but one of..
yea yea yea
i know the line
I wish to be alone
And i do not mind
What do you do when God is calling you higher
and assigning someone in your life to draw you nearer to him
through good and bad
for better or for worst?
Ive decided to run
run,run as fast as i can
you cant catch me I'm the….
lost and confused girl who never knew what love was because I
never received it from my family
I'm the 31 year old woman making excuses to not dig deeper
and confront my worst enemy
I'm the successful single mom who is alone, because i chose to
cut everyone off
why?
because I'm afraid to love
afraid to become vulnerable
and let someone get so close to my heart
that they could hear the very heart beat of my soul
wrestling with my desires, ambitions, hopes and strongholds

#12
My eyes were closed
I could not see
what the Lord said
that he had for me
My heart was
troubled
my spirit
consumed with
fear
because i thought i
was on my own
and no help was
near
i was overwhelmed
consumed in my
tasks and goals
of the visions i had
and my stories
untold
but God stepped in
and told me who i
was
he comforted my
heart
and extended his
unfailing love
he nourished my wounds
anointed my head with oil
gave me instruction
and encouraged me to walk in faith
Amen

Fight
/fīt/
verb/noun
1. Fiercely and intently grabbing hold of time.

Helpmate
I am a woman
taken from a man
the word says we came from his rib
i want you to understand.
woman came from man
not man from woman
although both are needed to get God's Plan done on the
earth.
God didn't see fit for man to be with out a helper
But why do we as woman, manipulate the man?
is it to maintain our independence?
to control him?
to be relevant?
a woman is there to help.

Awaken
I was created
not replicated
never intimidated
of who I'm destined to be
broken into pieces shattered and torn
thats where you will find your jewels to adorn
cast out
but not broken
shook and awoken
to who and what I'm assigned to

My world
i see pink flowers
i feel pink shades of sun rays
i smell pink blossoms
i hear sweet nothings
i taste exotic succulents
i see pink clouds
i feel pink wind
i smell pink cookies
i hear children
i taste honest fables
i see pink lights
i feel pink heat
i smell pink tea
i hear large feet
i taste painful thorns

Gold
is refined under the highest temperature
brewing, boiling out all impurities as the heat rises
Gold is stirred, and tossed around to become Gold
Gold
everyone desires it
its value
its status
few are willing to go through the process of becoming
Gold
or to create it.
Many people look for the easiest way out
they buy it
trade it
collect it
but none of these compare in matriculating through the
process of
of becoming
Gold

Refreshing

There is a refreshing in my soul
there is restoration begging to unfold
there is a reward for the diligent work our hands have
forgone
i can feel it
it begins to manifest in the fruits of your heart
the fruit that the bible speaks of
those of long suffering, kindness- and JOY
i can feel it
i can see it
in myself
you walk different
you speak differently
you extend compassion
you know who you are
why you were created.
refreshing
isn't it?
to know what you've been called to
to know why you exist
its not just to multiply and acquire assets
but to reflect God's Glory in the earth
He deserves all, the praise
he is worthy.
How refreshing…
to know who controls every step I take
every word i speak
every idea i create
I surrender those things to him and become
refreshed.

Broken Hearted
The broken hearted
is a price divine
A place where God can meet you
to unveil what is truly broken
Broken hearted
how sweet your pain
When God comes to heal your heart again
Broken heart
what a delight
to have God mend what this world has done
It isn't until you are broken
and realize your state thereof
Where God can meet you
and began to bring you higher
to impart in you,
who you really are
He has wiped my tears
with his right hand of power and love
healed my wounds that no other could treat
picked up my head when all i felt was defeat
Because we wouldn't allow for him to step in our lives
until we realized
that we are indeed
broken

HeartBREAKER

A man once told me i would be a heart breaker
i looked at him and laughed because at that age i didn't
like boys
but now I'm grown— — —
and i can say
i have broken many hearts
the first was in college
it was an innocent love
but he went to a different college
and i didn't do long distances
he always yearned for me
over the miles apart
i met his family
they thought we would never depart
but we did.
and i became engrained in his mind
as the one that got away.
But then,
I was sure i found love
it was more of an obsession
he was controlling
followed me everywhere
then eventually—-
he became abusive
he has a restraining order on him till this day.
boyfriend number 3
he was quite a delight
from a foreign land
and like to stay out all night
eventually
that grew old for me

as i desired to have more
i caught him dancing
one night with a——
anyway
i decided to become rebellious
and not settle down
i had a lot of fun
with this one guy
and now he is my BD
funny how that works
when you decide to say
"Imma just do me"
-NOT
Ive broken other hearts,
not that I'm keeping score
but what I've come to realize,
is that i was the one with a broken heart.

Sought Out
Through all the mess i put myself through
you never left
in all the bad decisions i made
you managed to keep me in good health
In all of my search of wanting to fill my hole
you waited patiently, your so divine
i ran, i walked i turned my heart away from you
but you continually sought me the entire time
when i finally gave up
and came to the end of myself
you taught me who i was
you walk with me
you comfort me
in you i find perfect love

1:32 AM
its 132
not 123
at these times i imagine
who i will eventually be
i get the most work done
my mind is so clear
i can prepare for my day
as it begins to draw near
132 now turns 134
not long before 2
and then ill begin to count down the hours until
i am no longer allowed to fall back asleep
its 135
25 minutes away
I'm wondering if I can fall back to sleep today
just 30 more seconds from a minute away
136
more than half way there
when I'm done writing this poem
i pray that i am settled
that i accept the fact that i need another 4 hours of sleep.

Reflections of my affliction
In my most painful years
I learned the most
I was focused
Determined
Strong
perserving
until I pushed into my next level
In these afflictions
God did his best work
He would cut somethings off
add more substance
show me myself
and I'm thankful for it all
Its true that all things work together for your good
The good and the bad
Without the bad you wouldn't be able to evolve
evolving is necessary
though uncomfortable
 painful
sorrowful
and many other things
Its all worth it in the end.

Glow
Im glowing, Im glowing
His love in me is flowing
Im growing, and glowing
The grace from him is showing
Im sowing and glowing
His Mercy is ever overthrowing
the lies and facades of my former self.
Im glowing Im glowing
His righteousness is overflowing
Im glowing and showing
to know him manifests this Glow

Unnamed.
Unbothered.
resolved.
Unannounced
uninhibited
and of a sound mind.
unashamed
unblamed
blameless
abiding
in his steadfast love.
untouched
unmoved.
perfected in him.
his name, above all names.
In Jesus Name.

Flood
Its flooding
His sprit has poured out
upon us
upon this place
while praises went up in the sanctuary
his wind blew
over me
i felt the rain fall down from heaven
it soaked me
and flooded the sanctuary
i stood still
so i wouldn't fall
I stood in the puddles
in the river
of his flood
Then I opened my eyes.

Clouds

Clouds are beautiful in the sky
each varying in its own way
some are pink
some are gray
some turn colors throughout the day
some look fluffy
some look tall
some make different shapes
that no one can recall
Most importantly
is what clouds can do
They shelter us and lead us
when no one has a clue
They pour out new blessings upon the earth
encouraging fruit and vegetation
its no wonder why people can create whatever they desire
from the source of an imagination.

Refuge

I was out
in the open all alone
But God kept me beneath his arms
I was ostracized, humiliated with a torn identity
But God came in and told me who I ought to be
I was rejected, abused, cursed and damned
But God came in and taught me who I am
I shed many tears, excelled to be seen
But God said to place my trust and hope in him.
Everyone must go through these facets of life
I pray that one day you will get it right
To slow down and listen
to what God has for you.
If you don't know your agenda
the world will give you something to do.
Be strong and encouraged in your daily tasks
God is such a gentlemen and will give you exactly what
you ask
He chastens those that he loves
so count it an honor
then before you know it you wont be able to recognize
yourself.

LORD

When you think its over
God says it has just begun
Some situations appear dead
but God said he has overcome
He will let our hearts become broken
and our spirits disdained
just to come in our midsts
and be God again
In all of our pain
he has extended hope
filled us with his spirit
and allowed us to cope
My Lord My Savior
there is no one like you
I don't deserve this love we share
But I am grateful that we do
You don't let a day or night go by
without showing and expressing your love
I pray everyone may see you
As you descend like a dove

Meekness
is an attribute that we all need
its not a fruit readily available
but one of the most important indeed
God desires us to be
submissive in his instructions
with a posture of grace and servitude
he commands us to be teachable, patient and humble
Help us Lord
to answer this call
to put ourselves aside
and be long-suffering in it all

Fragmented
discontent
that was the state that i was in
fragmented
my mind was everywhere
thats why i was unproductive and inefficient
fragmented
disheartened
why is it that
God allow
others to tear
you down ?
when your
unable or too
young to fend
for yourself
fragmented
love shattered
thats what i
became
fragmented
a broken mess
as i glued myself together with shattered pieces
fragmented
dark despair
is what i felt
with gaps and holes of the pieces glued together
fragments
fragment
fragmented

Faith
is the
evidence of things unseen.
hoped for, and desired.
it tries your character
and identifies what you are really made of.
What is your posture
when things are not as they seem.
Thats when it's time to hope in the evidence of things
unseen.
an application of faith
in any situation
will make everything ok
if we could only stay still in the presence of God
and obey.

I Love pink Flowers
the love of flowers
i love flowers
pink roses to be exact
i admire their beauty
as they help me to relax
they encourage me that one can still be beautiful and
elegant
in the midst of death
and that some of the most admirable things in life have
thorns
uncomfortable to hold or to touch
I really love the pink ones
because they all smell
pretty
there sweet smell, fresh fragrance
of things that are to be
i close my eyes and take a whiff
not knowing if they will ever smell exactly as they just did
in the next moment or day

Illumination

bright light
white light
alls right
when God is in sight
dimmed light
dark light
nothings's right
all is gone
electrical light vs
sunlight
manmade vs God laid

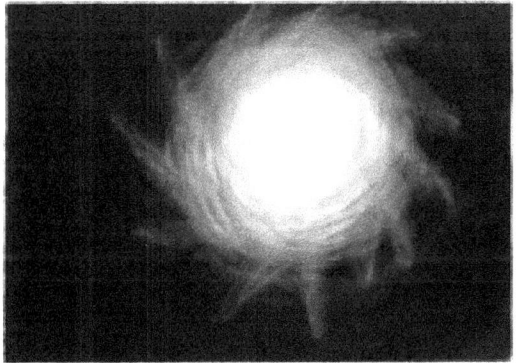

Light stimulates sight
just a little while longer
until your breakthrough surfaces
so never give up, you could be right on the edge.
just a little while longer
Until God serves justice
to the injustices you went through
at an uncontrollable hand

Shift
just a little longer
the rain is slowing down
the sun will come out and nourish every living organism
just a little while longer
just as the sunsets
and the day closes out
until God awards us with another
just a while longer
when you find out
that ALL things are working together for your good
just a while longer when you will see God shift
your worst enemies and foes
he will assist
into prophetic alignment
opening your bright future

The confession of my MAN obsession

I have a confession
and I pray it set you free
for me,
I had been blind to this detail of my life
But God has given me wisdom to see
God is such a gentlemen when it come to our deliverance
and Im thankful, sincerely so
If you told me this about myself sooner
I'm not sure how this story may have been told
All my life I have had perverse relationships with men
since I was a little girl
and when I say perverse, Im referring to the misguided and
perverted images created
around the subject thereof,
at any rate
It began with my Stepdad,
the character flaws and the acts of molestation toward me
caused me to lose a lot of respect for him
my biological dad was never there,
he was addicted to crack my entire life
NOW, God has showed me THIS is why
I could never keep or honor a relationship with a man
No matter the role-
mentor, lover, so on and so forth
But I ask you this now,
Have you been forced into this situation as well?
Have you allowed yourself to heal?
have you ever confronted it within yourself?
or have you went on with life, like me thinking everything
would be ok
and go through one failed relationship after the other?
that was my story, I am determined to be FREE
The devil can not have my future and who I am destined to
be.
I pray you come to this resolve as well.

Determine what you could afford
Be content in who you are called to be
not wishing anyone else's life
Be free
to walk in the design of your creator
if you compare yourself to others
you are liable to become a hater
The reality is no one's life is better than yours
some of the most extravagant and fruitful lives
are embedded under a sea of monsters
and poisonous plants galore
These words may seem fleeting
if your not quite there or here
but remember there is no one
with whom you should compare
Everyone has a price
determine what you could afford

Still standing or Standing still
Standing in one place
isn't staying still at all
while your standing
the world is revolving
others are evolving
some are stuck too
standing still, in one place
does no one any good
your not going back nor forward
and everyone around laughs
I knew they would
Standing in one place
gets boring after a while
you have the same view
the same experience
of the same days previously recorded
standing in one place
guarantees that you wont amount to anything
have you ever asked yourself or pondered
why are you still standing
seriously why are you still standing
do you wish to be progress?
if you get the balls to take your first step
You will begin to see
that standing still was just a waste of time
unless you were just taking a break to recollect your
thoughts

Masque
Green clay masks
Every week
at the end of the week
I like to prepare a mask
made of green clay from Europe or France
with a few drops of my favorite essential oil
lavender and tea tree oil to be exact
Some people prepare masks daily
Anyway, I mix it in my bowl
and apply it to my face
it pulls out impurities and
softens fine lines and reduces wrinkles

Star light, stars bright
up in the sky on this dark night
wonder why other stars don't shine as you do
Stars may shine brighter in the presence of dimmer stars
but from where Im positioned, it seems as if one
is simply brighter than the other
Star light, stars bright
wonder if the dimmer star
is bothered by the other star's light
as some people are in the world

Restricted
I was restricted
from my painful wounds
obtained while traveling through this obstacle called life
restricted
I was restricted in my movement
the movement of laughter, love, and forgiveness
restricted and constricted
restricted and paralyzed
restriction
what could break it?
nothing but the Love of God
which surpasses all understanding
His love is unfailing

Seasoned into a year
Spring, summer, winter -fall
not long before
a year goes by
Winter, fall, spring-summer
where will your life and dreams be?
Summer, winter, fall and spring
as the time passes
you will begin to slumber
fall, spring, summer, winter
not long before another
year go by

#44

Have you ever been afraid for your life
hoping that when you fell asleep
that nothing or no one would attack you
rape or molest you
i have been
left to fend for your self, on your own
have you
I've said its not fair
but in that time, i didn't care
i just wanted to be free
have you ever felt
betrayed, or misused, abandoned and rejected
i have
i know what thats like
Im glad I was headstrong
and chose to fight
fight for my mindset
my future, my goals
God helped me.
He could help you
if you chose to heal
and make everything anew
if you made the decision
to not be a victim, to not be weak
to not ingest the poison that the Devil tried to make you
drink

Butterflies
flying high
upon the leaves
across the sky
soaring to find
the pleasure for
today.
butterfly free as
ever
depending upon the
weather
where will your next
destination be?
butterfly
took a break
and landed on a leaf
just to asses the
coordinates.

FREE
/frē/
adj.
1. It means no strings attached; no chains.

Pantomath
I thought I knew everything
all of the time
i never let anyone else talk
because, i already knew the answer
I thought i knew everything
i wanted control
i didn't want to listen to anyone
i never followed where others would go
i thought i knew everything
it turned out I did know a lot
but there was so much more than what, i thought i knew
I've realized,
that i don't know everything
that i need others
there perspectives, experiences advice and so much more
i learned to listen
previously i only heard
so that I could know everything

Pretty.
pretty girl, pretty girl
there is no other like you
when you look into the mirror
do you see you
pretty girl, pretty girl
smile a little more
the world is yearning for your
light
the days are coming forth
pretty girl, pretty girl
has anyone told you your
pretty today
a stranger, a boyfriend, or
lover or maybe another would
you say
pretty girl, pretty girl
why are you always so down
hoping, wishing and dreaming
you were someone else
pretty girl, pretty girl
i have one last thing to say
will you ever think you are pretty
although the world says so everyday?
-Inspired by a pretty girl

Seven
1234567
the number of completion
7654321
the countdown
until he come
7
its perfect
the number i mean
there are 7 heavenly bodies in the presence of God
Daily.
7 trumpets will blow
then there will be no more
1
2
3
4
5
6
7
completely and utterly complete
seven-
My guide, my friend
my comforter
he held my hand
on the night of my deliverance
seven
I see him daily, reminding me that I'm not alone
in 7 bars i completed this poem.

Noted
At some point you figure out life is much more than you
your dreams and goals
and the only reason why you remain on earth is to fulfill
a purpose.
that God has designed for you to accomplish
I believe you will come like the rain

Instructions

The lord spoke to me
He said the time is drawing near
he said make sure you are in order
and do not fear
The lord spoke to me
he said say what i say
he told me he would put the words in my mouth day by day
the lord spoke to me
he told me to love and forgive my enemies
because the time is drawing near and there is no time to
waste

Broken trees,broken limbs
does it matter who helps put me back together again
those that are broken, those that are weak,
some who have strength, others that are meek
when your limbs are broken
who help you to put yourself back together again?
does it mater?
that it may not be a friend
'if in the end you were put back together".

In the fire
I was placed
to burn a painful death
God kept me in the midst thereof
no other could save me from
My enemies watched in awe to see
their evil acts had no affect on me
I knew If I stood on his word
he would perform and preserve
He kept me in each waking minute
whenever i was afraid
i closed my eyes and remembered his promises
as i began to pray
I closed my eyes and travelled back
from where he brought me from
I knew in that moment if i simply believed
He would give me the strength to overcome
Overcome whatever the enemy put up against me
The truth is God has already won
In the midst of Life's fires
Remember where God has brought you from.

Hey Dad
good morning how are you?
I get your texts everyday
but that will never replace all the years you were never
there
I know you said you were on drugs
and couldn't help me much
but most times i just don't care
i was left in the arms of a strange man while you were
gone
who God could only keep me from
still had to undergo the pains and trials
of not really being loved by anyone
The truth is doing drugs is a selfish act
because to do it, you would only have to care about
yourself
i know-because many times i had the urge to go there
myself'
But then i remembered
that i cant let my son down
i cant lose everything i worked so much for
but most of all, i couldn't be like you
Don't get me wrong i still love you
and the efforts you put forth
but nothing and no one will be able to fix the 26 years you
weren't there.

Power
Looking through a fog
I couldn't see clear
Because Ive given my life to christ
He has always been near
What do you do
when your'er told to walk ahead
but you can not see your feet
what do you say to yourself
when all thats in sight is defeat
As for me I close my eyes
and I hear a small still voice say
take this next with me
and I will guide you along the way
It is the voice of God
that travels with me
through the waking hours
when you master this love walk
He will give you all POWER

The equation of you
Embrace
being the one who doesn't fit in
who isn't first to be called
and who doesn't play to win
because there is a reward in being just who you are
embrace being misunderstood, judged and criticized
because it isn't up to your critics
on how much you succeed or gain in this life
always do what God said
no matter the faces, no matter the shade and no matter the
places
because obedience is better than sacrifice as the word
said
What I'm saying is not fitting in means your doing
something right
it means your called out and you should position yourself
for flight.
after all eagles soar alone

Single and not ready to mingle
Single life isn't so bad
it will give you a chance to learn of things you are worthy to
have
it teaches you how to love and date yourself
it teaches you your strengths and weaknesses
and where you really need help.
Many people don't like to be alone
At this time, if thats you
I would encourage you to seek the areas to where you are
strong
these are the clues
for true healing and revelation to take place in your soul
this is the area where others over compensate for an
offense thereof
I pray this makes sense to you
single life is about identifying who you are and what your
able to offer
not only to God but if you look forward to getting married
one day
what you can offer.
A great man once said your not ready to get married if you
cant put yourself before your other half
thats the measuring device to whether you are truly ready
to become yoked.
As for me-
I enjoy who I am
What I'm doing
and i am most certainly not ready to put someone else
above
my dreams, desires and ambitions
so for now,
I am enjoying my space of singleness

He loves me?
He loves me not?
he is only capable of loving me
the way he loves everything else
I heard him say he loved me
but his actions showed otherwise
The reality is,
He loved me not.
Do I love me?
To stand upon my value
of who God said I am
Even if that meant being alone until...
not forever but whenever
I arrived to a place of wholeness
and stood firm on not compromising.
because I wanted company.

I AM happy this is true
and nothing can keep me from shining
IM full of ambition and passion
So I always push into my next level
Once you get over the hump called trauma
you begin to live
living without remnants of guilt and shame from your past.
I am experiencing true freedom.
There are a lot of experts giving advice and prescribing
pills
but at the end of the day its your decision to stop self
medicating
and to allow your wounds to naturally heal.

Vision
A visionary
is not customary
never ordinary
but just plain real.
never making excuses, sacrifices for those they love
and is always 2 steps ahead.
the visionary
usually misunderstood, ostracized and placed with high
demands
they only hold a few to understand.
their mind,intricacies and future goals.
The visionary, usually a vision
in themselves
constantly evolving while those around gaze in awe.
A visionary
is not customary
never ordinary
but just plain real.

Diamonds & Pearls
Oh to be a diamond or pearl
buried beneath the earth
lost in the sea
brewing in the highest temperatures
that no man could observe or see
growing over the billions of years
It took to make you who you are

He know best
I use to ask myself-Why me
for many years i could not understand.
After many years of pain and non progressiveness
I believed i had bad luck
since nothing in my life ever worked out the way i planned
and sacrificed for
But then God stepped in
and he showed me, he wanted me to get to the end of me
and i mean
me trying to fix it
saying well if i made more money than this
or if i sacrificed for this long
or if i obtained this additional degree or license then this
but what i have grown to learn
is that God wanted me to move out of the way
so that he can step in and
Be the God who he is today
the provider
a healer
a comforter
and so much more
once i understood his provisions
i understood that God knows best
and now the best is yet to come
not because of me, but because i know
it is him working through me
his yielded vessel

Total cost (TC)
There is an infestation
of ill minded individuals trying to circumvent
the design that God has for your life
They know not what they do
However, I can assure you
even there initial intentions
are not good
God will allow them to come in your area of influence
just to show you yourself in your process
not knowing this, will cost you.

Waste not
Please do not waste my time
but me wasting my time
would be,
me allowing you to waste my time
so excuse me
as i exit stage left
exiting
from your drama, tragedy, satire
of a play
where nothing goes right
and i have nothing else to say

Pride

Missing you is poison to me
I hate to reminiscence of what we could be.
So I stop myself.
Hoping you were different is a waste of time
As it turned out we didn't want the same things so I've left
you behind.
You told me we had a future and all
Your pride is too steep, and thats why you've had a great
fall
Down, down you go until your humbled enough
I pray someone is there to encourage you
and that you will never give up
until you reach the fruition
of what I always saw in you
but since your not there
all i can say is good luck.

#Queening

A King calls and choses his queen
He finds her
He courts her
He desires to fulfill all of the desires of her heart.
Not the other way around
He doesn't threaten her to accept his request
She knows, with every bone in her body
Never doubting if he is the one
second guessing and making excuses
for a lack thereof
Very similar to how God calls us into fellowship with him
Nothing can feel as good as that
being thought of, loved for,
understanding all of your intricacies
when you think of dating from this perspective
things become clearer
of who and who not to entertain.
waiting until my King draws me into his presence
with his scepter, like Esther.

light stimulates sight
just a little while longer
until your breakthrough surfaces
so never give up, you could be right on the edge.
just a little while longer
Until God serves justice
to the injustices you went through
at an uncontrollable hand

Sexual tensions
are rising in me
i suppress my thoughts i just want to be free
funny how we enslave ourselves and then make excuses
I have to maintain my posture in order to breakthrough
sexual tensions
what are they exactly?
Just the evidence of my inability of self control
I will meditate on Gods word
instead of calling Joe Schmo
Because the reality is the incident isn't worth my audience
with God
or even allowing for some random guy to have my body.
Its quite disgusting actually.
I cant fathom having some random guy touch me or even
interchanging sex
funny how what use to be so familiar is now completely
foreign.
and just like that sexual tensions are gone.

Newness

A new you calls for action to take
new equipment to carry
new realities to face
A new you demands for the old you to die
to die a painful death that may take forever to subside
a new you requires that you surround yourself with people
who is nothing like you
nothing like your old friends
and requires something previously unlike you
that you must do
being made anew sounds catchy and cliche
but to truly be made anew
there would be no more words to say
other than
I wanted more than I was so i sacrificed to be anew.

Thankful
I am thankful from where the Lord have brought me from
no more languishing over bad things
hoping that I had made decisions from my past.Thankful
Im thankful I'm not sitting around
unable to do anything because i don't know who i am
Like so many others
thankful that i don't complain and dread doing what i do
everyday
thankful to shine in the way God wishes to display
Im thankful
Thankful that the Lord chose me
to be an ambassador for his plan, purpose and his perfect
thing
Thankful, that he has cultivated a heart in me to be
obedient and trust him no matter what
Im thankful
Im encouraged
Im inspired.

Unconditional Love
Sometimes I feel selfish
for wanting to do me
Knowing that God has spared me
to do his will
knowing that he was patient
until i reach maturation in the understanding of who i am
but yet I still want to do me
i cant help it
i pray for his forgiveness
he show me that he is still there
and that he loves me unconditionally
no other love i know like this
i know that he will never change
and will let everything and everyone fall to the waist side
until i understand
that we will always pick up where I left off

Perfectly imperfect
I can not be without you
nor exist without you
breath without you
live without you
I need you
every waking hour
because I am incapable
of maintaining my very existence
you know everything
i can hide nothing from you
you know all my secrets and idiosyncrasies
teach me the way that I should go
put the words in my mouth
and help me to say NO
to the things you would prefer not for me to experience
I know that I'm not perfect
and because you are who you are
you always perfectly work in
the imperfectness in me
More than half way there…

Jesus
He came to do the Father's will
and whomever believed they would be healed
He is the key to Eternal Life
He has died to preserve our eternal lives
His wisdom never fails
His parables of life in every detail
will restore your mind and spirit
He is the key to life fulfilled
If you are evil you will never complete his will
His name is Jesus
the name above all names
The name by which every knee shall Bow
and know that he is Lord

Con·fi·dence
I am confident
becoming more confident
by the minute
in every stroke of every key that I type even in this moment
Because it is required
I have cultivated it
nurtured it
encouraged myself
In confidence
I must persist
it must exist
in every room that you enter
that I enter
if you truly desire to be your best self

Sugar
So good so sweat
high in calories
prone to disease
but it tastes so good
with everything it doesn't matter
but the repercussions for such an addictive
are deadly to many
but they don't care

Breakfast
I broke my fast at sunset
I guess I should have not done that
It reminds me of how i compromise in what i know i
shouldn't do
fasts promote self discipline and killing your fleshly desires
what I've found is that i make excuses to not go all the way
through
i say next week i will do better
and then when that day come i find another excuse
to push it off until later
steadily compromising on breakthroughs and audience
with God
The devil hates when we are committed to getting closer to
God
how long will we allow him to dissuade us
The master and king of lies
should we continue to compromise and bite the fruit
It will be to our demise
Psalm 119:93

#77
I rose early in the morning
To start my work
Went to bed late at night
Just to find the better me
Free of shame and guilt
Through being torn and fragmented
is where you learn strength and happiness
Digging, digging and digging
Until i uncovered the most precious stone
That the earth could create under pressure, heat and
depth
how ironic i guess
to know that your most painful experiences will bring forth
the most refined version of you
funny how miners dig for hours amongst dirt and coal
the deeper they go the more valuable the stone

Afterword

Love is light, and through it we are empowered to overcome the most incomprehensible darkness. God is love, and He commended His love towards us, in that, while were yet unchanged sinners, the Beautiful Son died for us. This book of "fragments" was birthed from the heart of God, to bring forth wholeness in the lives of the reader. Wholeness comes in pieces, and with wholeness comes peace of a kind that surpasses all knowledge.

Dr. Mark T. Jones Sr.

www.ingramcontent.com/pod-product-compliance
Lightning Source LLC
Chambersburg PA
CBHW071848020426
42331CB00007B/1913